3D

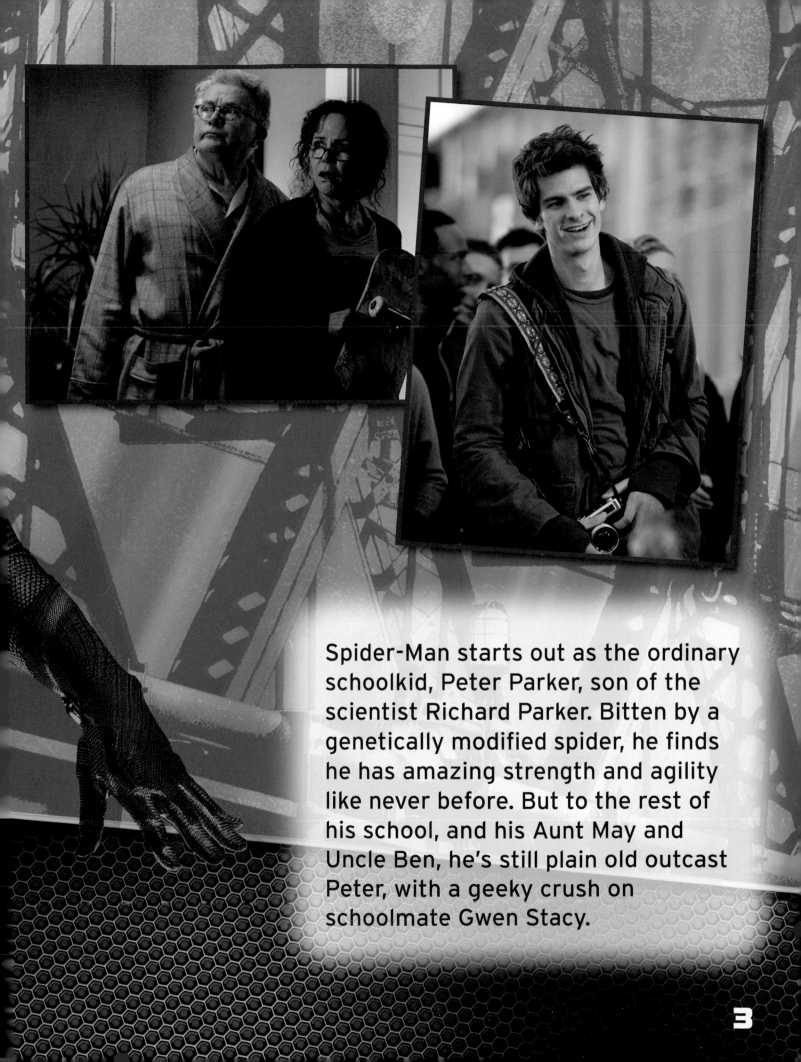

Spider-Man starts out as the ordinary schoolkid, Peter Parker, son of the scientist Richard Parker. Bitten by a genetically modified spider, he finds he has amazing strength and agility like never before. But to the rest of his school, and his Aunt May and Uncle Ben, he's still plain old outcast Peter, with a geeky crush on schoolmate Gwen Stacy.

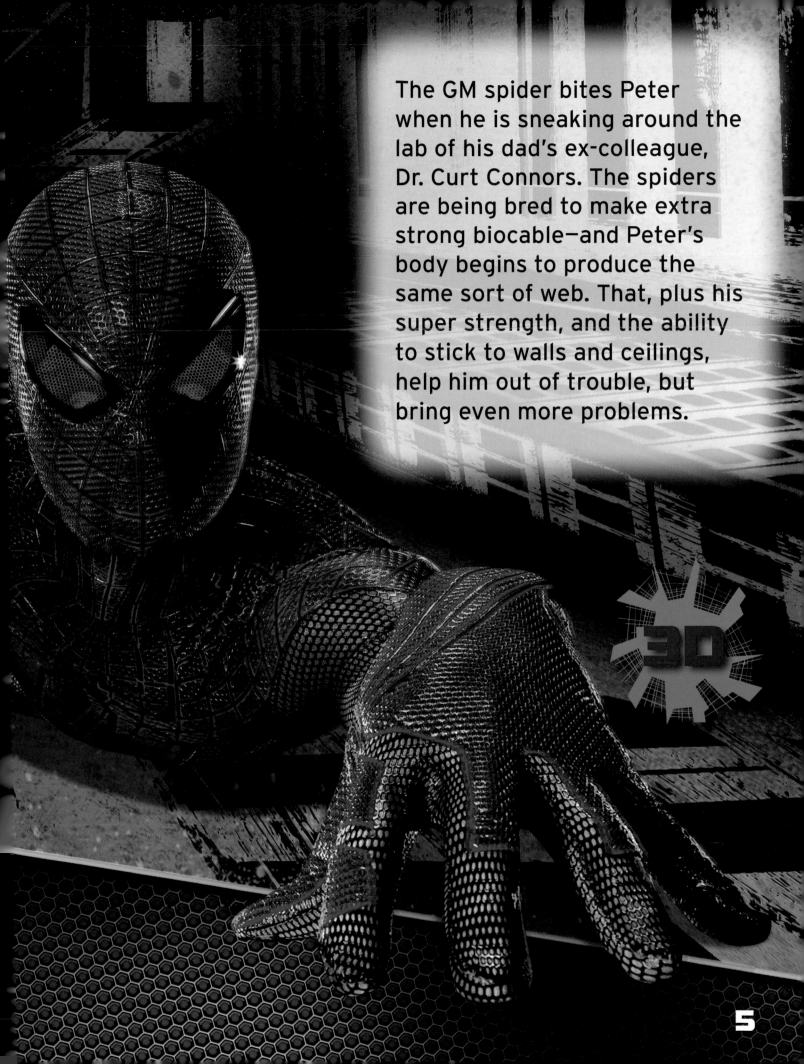

The GM spider bites Peter when he is sneaking around the lab of his dad's ex-colleague, Dr. Curt Connors. The spiders are being bred to make extra strong biocable—and Peter's body begins to produce the same sort of web. That, plus his super strength, and the ability to stick to walls and ceilings, help him out of trouble, but bring even more problems.

Life doesn't get easier for Peter once he discovers his new talents. He seems to find thugs and thieves at every turn, and his Uncle Ben gets caught in the crossfire. Determined to get revenge, Peter creates a new Super Hero costume, complete with wrestling mask and tight-fitting suit. He harnesses his body web to use in his web-shooters, his own invention using old wristwatches.

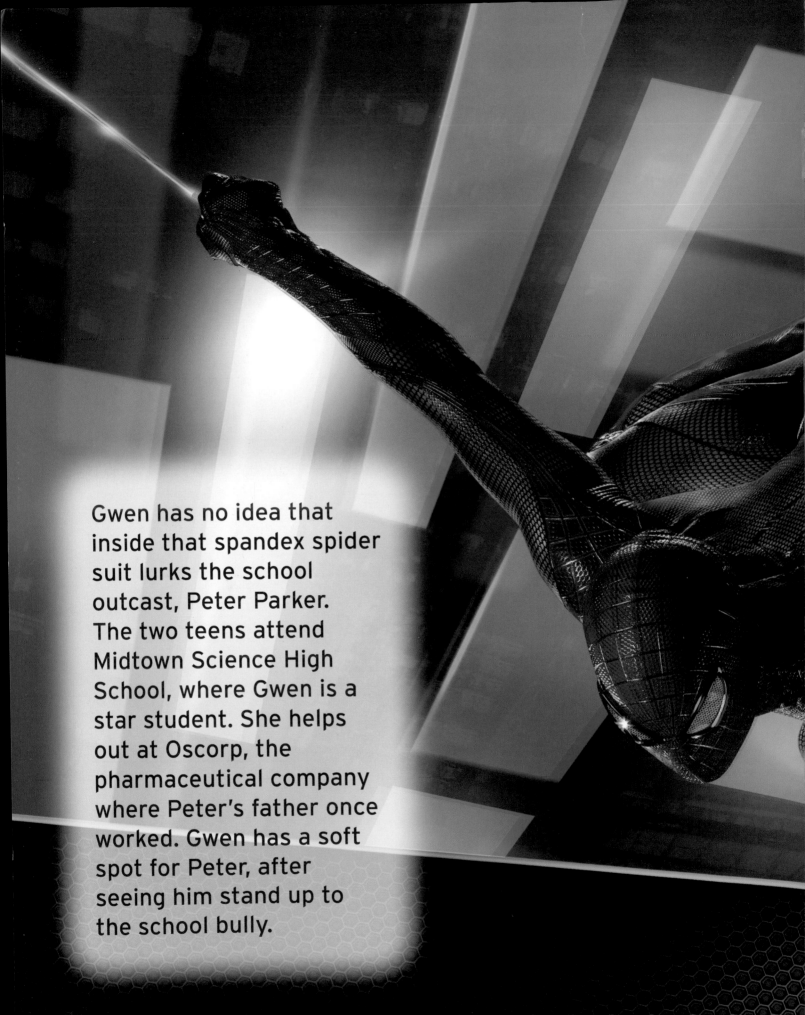

Gwen has no idea that inside that spandex spider suit lurks the school outcast, Peter Parker. The two teens attend Midtown Science High School, where Gwen is a star student. She helps out at Oscorp, the pharmaceutical company where Peter's father once worked. Gwen has a soft spot for Peter, after seeing him stand up to the school bully.

THE AMAZING
SPIDER-MAN™

3D

So, who is Spider-Man's new enemy? He's known as the Lizard, and is the mutated reptilian form of Dr. Curt Connors. Dr. Connors was once Richard Parker's partner at Oscorp. Under pressure from his boss, and threatened with losing his job, he injects his own limb-regeneration formula—and this is what happens!

3D

Dr. Connors knows how important it could be to perfect his regeneration serum. His own right arm is missing, after all. His superiors at Oscorp want to speed up the research to find a cure for their CEO. Connors injects himself as a trial but it isn't only his arm that changes... His whole body mutates until he becomes a nine-feet-tall reptile hybrid.

A hidden camera reveals the identity of Spider-Man, and the Lizard goes hunting for him at Peter's school. After a fight, Spider-Man learns that the whole island of Manhattan is in danger. The Lizard plans to release a lethal chemical cloud from the top of the Oscorp building.

Captain Stacy knows Peter as a friend of his daughter, Gwen Stacy. But when Peter tries to tip him off about who the Lizard really is, the police captain has Peter thrown out of his office. It isn't long before Stacy captures Spider-Man and discovers his real identity.